# JERRY
# RICE

*(Photo on
front cover.)*

**Jerry Rice
takes off
on a 51 yard
touchdown
pass from
Steve Young.**

*(Photo on
previous pages.)*

**Rice runs
after catching
a pass in a
game against
the Cincinnati
Bengals.**

Photography supplied by Wide World Photos Inc.

Library of Congress Cataloging-in-Publication Data
Rambeck, Richard.
Jerry Rice / Richard Rambeck.
p. cm.
Summary: Relates the football career of the receiver
for the San Francisco 49ers who scorded more touchdowns
than any other player in the history of the
National Football League.
ISBN 1-56766-204-8 (Lib. Bdg.)
1. Rice, Jerry—Juvenile literature. 2. Football players—
United States—Biography—Juvenile literature.
[. Rice, Jerry. 2. Football players. 3. Afro-Americans-
-Biography.]
I. Title
GV939.R53R36  1995                      95-6463
796.332'092 B—dc20                       CIP
                                          AC

# JERRY RICE

BY RICHARD RAMBECK

**S**teve Young went back to pass. The San Francisco 49er quarterback looked to the left, and then to the right, but he already knew where he was going to throw the ball. He was going to throw down the middle of the field, to receiver Jerry Rice. Young tossed the ball toward Rice in the end zone. Rice was covered by two Los Angeles Raiders defenders, but it didn't matter how many Raiders were around him. He was going to make this play!

**"W**hen the ball is in the air, it's mine," Rice said. "But I have to fight for it." Rice jumped over the two Raiders and caught the ball. He had scored another touchdown. But this one was special Rice had just scored the 127th TD of his pro career, the most ever scored by any player in the history of the National Football League. Rice set the touchdown record in San Francisco's first game of the 1994 season.

Rice is simply the best receiver ever to play the game. He has scored more TDs than anybody else, and has caught more touchdown passes than any other receiver. He was the NFL's Most Valuable Player in 1987. He was the MVP of the 1989 Super Bowl as the 49ers beat

8

Rice (80)
gets a ride
from 49er
tackle Steve
Wallace (74).

Cincinnati, and he caught three touchdown passes in the 1990 Super Bowl, which San Francisco won 55–10 over Denver. "I wanted to make a name for myself," Rice said. He certainly has.

Jerry Rice grew up in Mississippi, where he played high school football. Then he went to Mississippi Valley State, a tiny university in Itta Bena, Mississippi. In college, Rice's teammates called him "World." He was all-world, they said, because no one could stop him. In one game, Rice caught five touchdown passes. Later, San Francisco coach Bill Walsh saw a film of that game and quickly became a big Jerry Rice fan.

The 49ers had won the 1985 Super Bowl, but Walsh felt that they needed a receiver to make big plays—but not just any receiver. He felt that they needed Jerry Rice. San Francisco picked Rice in the first round of the 1985 NFL draft. Rice didn't play well at first, though, dropping 11 passes in the first 11 games of the 1985 season. The San Francisco fans started to boo the rookie receiver. "I hadn't been booed in all my life," Rice said.

Rice was trying too hard to make a big play. He wanted to score a touchdown each time he went out for a pass.

*Rice holds onto the ball under pressure.*

"He'd be the first to admit that every time he touched the ball that first year, he wanted to go all the way," said San Francisco quarterback Joe Montana. "And you can't do that, although JR can come pretty close." Rice practiced with Montana and worked on catching the ball every time. His work soon paid off.

Late in the 1985 season, the 49ers played the Washington Redskins. Jerry Rice had the game of his life, catching ten passes for 241 yards and a touchdown. Nobody would ever worry about Rice dropping passes again! He was on his way to becoming a star. In 1986, Rice caught 86 passes for 1,570 yards and 15 touchdowns. His yardage total was the third highest in NFL history. In 1987, Rice scored an amazing 23 touchdowns.

After only three seasons in the NFL, Jerry Rice had become the most feared receiver in the game. Nobody made more big plays than the 49er star. Not only was Rice a great pass catcher, he was also a great runner after he caught the ball. "So many receivers want to catch the pass and find a place to lie down," said San Francisco tight end Jamie Williams. "Rice doesn't have a lot of fear. His main thing is getting to the end zone."

**A**ctually, Rice didn't have any fear at all. He would go anywhere to catch a pass — even to parts of the field filled with defenders. Many receivers are afraid of getting hurt if they have to catch passes in the middle of the field. "I don't mind going across the middle," Rice said. "It's a challenge to see if you can go across the middle and still come out in one piece. I feel like the fun is just starting after I catch the ball."

**I**n the 1989 Super Bowl against Cincinnati, the 49ers needed Rice to make a lot of big plays. San Francisco was behind 13–6 in the fourth quarter, until

Montana hit Rice with a 14 yard touch-down pass, tying the game 13–13. After Cincinnati kicked a field goal, San Francisco needed to go more than 90 yards for the winning touchdown. Montana kept throwing the ball to Rice, and Rice kept making big plays.

*Rice eyes the ball as he waits for a Steve Young pass.*

**A**lthough Rice didn't catch the winning TD pass, he caught almost everything else. For the game, Rice had 11 receptions for 215 yards, tying the Super Bowl record for number of catches and breaking the Super Bowl record for total receiving yards. For his efforts, Rice was named Most Valuable Player of the game.

A year later, Rice set another Super Bowl record by grabbing three TD passes against Denver.

" Jerry Rice," said Dallas defensive back James Washington, "is the best receiver ever to play the game." A lot of players and coaches agree with Washington. "I just want to make plays," Rice said. "I play each game in my mind first. I know exactly what I'm going to do on Sundays." He's going to fight for every ball thrown to him, and then he's going to try to score. It's something he does better than anyone who has ever played the game.